Trichotillomania Disorder Cure: How to Overcome Hair Pulling For Life

Causes, Treatments and Workbook for
Kids, Teenagers and Adults
Step by Step Guide Book

Susan Shaw

Table of Contents

Introduction

Hair loss is a normal occurrence. It happens when our scalps naturally shed hair. It also happens if we experience certain conditions that cause hair loss as a direct symptom.

Sometimes, hair loss happens due to psychological factors rather than biological factors. The condition known as *trichotillomania* is one instance of hair loss that doesn't exactly occur due to only biological factors.

Trichotillomania is best known as the compulsive need to pluck out one's own hair on a consistent basis. This causes imminent and noticeable hair loss, in addition to distress, social and/or impairment of one's normal functions.

The *Diagnostic and Statistical Manual of Mental Disorders* classifies this disorder as an *impulse control disorder*, due to its acute characteristics. Currently it is considered an anxiety disorder, a new diagnosis that affects the available treatment options for people who have the condition. Interestingly enough, it's also considered a chronic condition that's considered difficult to treat.

Many people deal with impulsive disorders on a regular basis. Some people have easier ways of dealing with their compulsions than others. Trichotillomania represents one of many impulsive disorders that people have difficulty treating at all, regardless of the treatment options that they might have available to them.

In fact, a lot of people feel helpless when it comes to treating conditions like trichotillomania. Given the tricky nature of stopping impulsive hair loss, people who suffer from the condition need assistance figuring out how to manage the condition and, eventually, overcome it.

That's where this book comes in. *Trichotillomania: Treatments and Cures for Children and Adults ~A Guide For Demystifying, Treating and Managing Trichotillomania* is a book designed to help people learn more about trichotillomania while, at the same time, learning how to cope and manage their disorder.

Within the course of the book, we want to present enough information for you to understand what it means to successfully manage and overcome the severe symptoms of this disorder.

In this book, you will:

- Learn about trichotillomania – the causes, symptoms, diagnoses and how it affects different parts of the body.
- Learn about trichotillomania's different treatments for children, teens and adults.
- Learn about alternative treatments that help people successfully treat the condition.
- Learn how psychotherapy helps people develop a strategy to help manage their trichotillomania.
- Learn how to prevent trichotillomania and stay motivated on a trichotillomania recovery program.

Trichotillomania: Treatments and Cures for Children and Adults ~ A Guide For Demystifying, Treating and Managing Trichotillomania will also give you advice about how to manage trichotillomania, in addition to resources to help you stay motivated on your recovery plan.

So, I want to thank you and congratulate you for downloading the book, *Trichotillomania: Treatments and Cures for Children and Adults*.

This book contains proven steps and strategies on how to Demystify, Treat and Manage Trichotillomania.

Thanks again for downloading this book, I hope you enjoy it!

Chapter 1: Behind Trichotillomania: The What, How And Why

Trichotillomania is a condition defined by developing the impulse to twist and pull out one's hair. In some cases, people develop a compulsive urge to eat their hair after yanking it out. The continual pulling (or eating) of hair eventually leads to noticeable hair loss, which then can lead to noticeable stress, social and/or impairment of one's normal behaviors.

As mentioned, the *Diagnostic and Statistical Manual of Mental Disorders* classified trichotillomania as an impulse control disorder, but a recent update changed the classification to an anxiety disorder, affecting how trichotillomania is treated in most cases.

When you think about it, trichotillomania isn't defined by a physical or mental illness. It's mainly defined by the repetitious behaviors.

This particular condition is widespread, even though it doesn't manifest in most people. Some people who have the disorder don't even realize they're suffering from it, until they see their symptoms match some of the characteristic symptoms of trichotillomania. That usually comes after their doctor diagnoses their strange behaviors, repetitious hair pulling or hair loss, as a symptom of other conditions.

Why You Might Have Trichotillomania... And Why You Might Not

Many people assume that their hair loss is due to a condition like trichotillomania. In most cases, it isn't. Sometimes, the symptoms from conditions like these manifest in ways that make us assume that's the case.

Trichotillomania is a 'self induced, continual loss of hair.' It's also defined as:

> *hair pulling with a growing sense of tension before pulling hair and gratification (relief) when and/or after pulling the hair.*

Some who have the condition don't experience trichotillomania in ways similar to others who have certain types of symptoms, including those symptoms best characterizing the condition.

Some people, for example, don't experience the rising tension and subsequent gratification or relief associated with the condition. In many cases, they don't realize that they've experienced those particular symptoms, since those actions are more or less intrinsic at that point.

Defining Trichotillomania

We already know trichotillomania is a type of impulsive disorder, however, some resources have different interpretations of trichotillomania as a medical condition.

Some sources place trichotillomania on the obsessive compulsive spectrum, which encompasses obsessive-compulsive disorder, skin picking (dermatillomania), nail biting (onychophagia), eating disorders and tic disorders.

Though, the similarities usually end there. Trichotillomania inherently possesses symptoms, neural functions and a cognitive profile different from the aforementioned compulsive disorders. So, what similarities does trichotillomania possess when compared to these disorders? Those similarities include:

- A tendency to have an urge to perform unwanted repetitive behaviors.
- An association with the behaviors of other compulsive disorders, such as obsessive-compulsive disorder.
- Symptoms including, but not limited to, having the inclination to repeat unwanted repetitive behaviors due to a psychological reason (and usually not a mental or physical reason).

Besides holding over those similarities, trichotillomania is present in several age groups. The condition is known to manifest in young children, pre-adolescents, young adults and adults.

→ Is trichotillomania a deliberate disorder?

Deliberate implies there's an inclination to repeat the behavior over time. People who experience trichotillomania may not consciously understand that they're doing the action (pulling out their hair) until they're doing it. This is usually best described as an automatic action, where they do the action without 'pre-screening' the action before it's performed (otherwise known as an unconscious action). While many people do experience unconscious hair removal episodes, many people have focused, otherwise deliberate, episodes of yanking out their hair. This usually happens when they desire to feel relief from yanking out their hair to specifically relieve a certain sensation originating from that action. So, when you look at it that way, trichotillomania, in some aspects, can be a deliberate disorder.

Usually, people who have trichotillomania talk to someone, typically a medical professional, to get assistance with deciding the right 'course of action' to take with their treatment. This is necessary because it's important for providers and patients to understand how their (individual) trichotillomania works, in order to assign the right type of treatment.

The Development Of Trichotillomania: Who Gets Trichotillomania?

As an impulsive (compulsive) disorder, the causes of trichotillomania aren't exactly understood. To start, this condition is considered a chronic condition, meaning that people who develop it may very well keep the disorder for the rest of their lives.

Medical professionals do know, however, it affects as much as 4 percent of the population. That percentage is pretty large when you consider how many people live in this country and around the rest of the world.

Women are considered to develop the disorder more than men. Some sources presume that's due to the tendency of women to seek medical help more than men, and that many men may experience the disorder just as much as women do. Although speculation is that both men and women may experience this condition at similar rates.

→ The name, trichotillomania

The name, trichotillomania, was created by Francois Henri Hallopeau, a French dermatologist. It's taken from the Greek terms: *trich*, *till(en)* and *mania*, respectively meaning *hair*, *to pull* and *madness/frenzy*.

Trichotillomania, as mentioned, develops in young children, teenagers and adults. Depending on the age of the person who develops the condition, it may present in different ways.

Infants may develop trichotillomania, however it's said that the disorder often 'develops around age 9 to 13.' That means children from those ages usually develop the condition starting at and between those ages.

Let's look at **who gets trichotillomania** in more detail:

→ Young children – less than 5 years

Young children may develop trichotillomania, however the symptoms are often regarded as cases of mild hair tugging that are characteristic of behaviors exhibited by young children. Many young children tug their hair (unknowingly) when awake or when they're asleep. This condition is usually compared to nail biting and thumb sucking at this age, since many children who do show signs of trichotillomania end up stopping on their own.

→ Pre-adolescents and young adults

As mentioned, most children develop trichotillomania between the ages of 9 to 13 years old. Most children affected with trichotillomania at this age are usually female. That accounts for at least 70 to 90 percent of children affected with trichotillomania at that age. When the condition starts at this age, it generally manifests as a chronic condition. Some children develop rituals alongside their trichotillomania behaviors or symptoms, including the chewing or licking of their lips and eating their hair.

→ Adults

Adults who develop trichotillomania for the first time might have developed the condition as the result of experiencing another psychiatric illness. Sometimes, addressing the symptoms of their primary illness helps put a stop to their trichotillomania symptoms.

When trichotillomania develops in early childhood (under 5 years of age), it's usually a normal behavior that goes away without any intervention. Usually when young adults or adults develop trichotillomania, they need medical intervention to help resolve their immediate symptoms. Adults, in particular, may have to have a primary psychiatric condition treated alongside their trichotillomania.

Sometimes, secondary infections develop alongside trichotillomania, especially if the hair pulling is bad. They usually occur due to picking, scratching or damaging the skin of the scalp. Other complications associated with trichotillomania, however, are rare.

The Demographics Of Trichotillomania

Although relatively rare, the onset of its characteristic symptoms make trichotillomania a more common disorder in recent times. The disorder is known to affect as much as 1 to 4 percent of people across the country (the general population).

The disorder is known to occur as much as 3.4 percent of adult females, which is considered more often than adult males, as mentioned. As much as 1.5 percent of adult males are known to have contracted some form of trichotillomania.

Let's look more into how trichotillomania affects people across the United States.

According to epidemiological studies about the subject, trichotillomania is said to affect 'as many as 8 million people across the United States.' That accounts for all people who have been reported to have treatment for trichotillomania within the United States. People who have trichotillomania are known to deny having the disorder, especially if it causes them significant emotional distress.

Due to the emotional distress, many people don't seek professional assistance or intervention for the treatment of their disorder, which is what leads to the 'skewed' results in studies documenting the amount of people who have sought treatment for trichotillomania.

A study on college students (in the United States) found

that as much as 2 percent of the study pool had past or current symptoms relating to that of trichotillomania.

Though, the rate did fall to 0.6 percent when they were restricted to other related conditions, such as mental relief and tension. Without imposing those 'restrictions,' the rate of hair pulling among the study pool resulted in 1.5 percent for males, while 3.4 percent of females were found to have engaged in mild to severe hair pulling (trichotillomania).

As we've mentioned in the last few sections, trichotillomania can develop into a chronic disorder, especially if developed during adolescence. The disorder itself can last as long as a few weeks to a few decades. In many cases, the symptoms last for a lifetime.

Sometimes, the age of onset influences the area of the body where people inflict their compulsive hair picking. Younger trichotillomania sufferers were found to have yanked and/or compulsively removed their eyelashes more than older sufferers, who were more likely to pull out their pubic hairs.

Going by age demographics for this condition, the prognosis usually depends on the age of the patient, as expressed by the following:

- Children generally have an excellent prognosis, as the disorder doesn't last a long time for them.
- Adolescents have a guarded prognosis, as it manifests in severe ways if left untreated.
- Adults have a poor prognosis, since they usually 'inherit' the condition from their adolescence.

While the onset of trichotillomania development does have substantial evidence showing how severe the condition develops at certain ages, there's no real cause behind the condition itself.

What Increases The Risks Of Trichotillomania?

Trichotillomania has several risk factors that determine how the condition may develop in people. While they're not always the real reason why a person may develop trichotillomania, they provide some answers for the origin of the condition in many people:

- **Family history** – Genetics might play a role in trichotillomania development. People who have had a relative experience the disorder may end up developing the condition.
- **Age** – Trichotillomania generally develops before or during the early teens, between the ages of 9 to 13. After development during those ages, it often morphs into a lifelong problem. Infants, too, can develop tendencies to yank out their hair, but it's usually mild and goes away.
- **Positive reinforcement** – People who have trichotillomania usually feel a sense of relief after compulsively yanking out their hair, causing them to experience some form of euphoria each time they perform the compulsive action. In order to maintain those 'positive feelings,' they deliberately keep pulling out their hair to eliminate their negative feelings.

- **Negative emotions** – People who have trichotillomania use hair pulling as a way to stifle any uncomfortable and/or negative feelings, including tensions, stress and anxiety. Some people use it to eliminate their frustration or fatigue.
- **Other disorders** – Sometimes, trichotillomania may occur as the result of another disorder, such as depression, obsessive-compulsive disorder or anxiety.

As mentioned, more women are treated for trichotillomania than men, due to them choosing to see medical help sooner. Young boys and girls, on the other hand, seem to be equally affected by this particular disorder.

The Characteristics Of Trichotillomania

Trichotillomania was first described as a disorder back in the late 1800s. It was first described as hair pulling in literature of the time. By 1889, French dermatologist Francois Henri Hallopeau had coined the term *trichotillomania,* for later use in medical and general literature canon.

By the year 1987, trichotillomania was officially recognized in the *Diagnostic and Statistical Manual of the American Psychiatric Association,* specifically the third revised edition (DSM-III-R).

The characteristics of trichotillomania take it to 'many places,' as they say. But, when you look closer at the characteristics of the condition, they describe a condition that affects a lot of people in rather unique ways. Unique, as in those unique to how compulsive disorders work.

→ Trichotillomania and PTSD

Trichotillomania may have an association with PTSD, otherwise known as post-traumatic stress disorder. In fact, research regarding the relationship between both conditions suggests that people who have certain mental health disorders, such as the aforementioned, may be more susceptible to developing trichotillomania in some form.

Data regarding the relationship between trichotillomania and PTSD was uncovered by researchers at Skidmore College and Harvard Medical School (in cooperation with the Massachusetts General Hospital) who conducted a study on a group of patients at the trichotillomania clinic. During the study, the researchers asked the participants about their past traumatic exposures and any known symptoms of PTSD.

During the study, they found that at least 75 percent of the patients had 'experienced at least one traumatic event during their lives.' 19 percent of those patients met the criteria for a formal PTSD diagnosis. On an interesting note, that particular rate was considered higher than typical rates found among the general population, which makes sense, due to the concentrated selection of patients who had symptoms of the disorder in the study.

On another interesting note, the researchers found that the severity of patients' experiences with trichotillomania were associated with milder symptoms of post-traumatic stress disorder. That may also indicate that they may have used trichotillomania to reduce anxiety, tension and stress linked to their PTSD symptoms.

Despite that, it doesn't mean that the patient's use of trichotillomania helps relieve their PTSD symptoms. The automatic (unconscious) behaviors, in addition to some focused (conscious) behaviors, of trichotillomania may serve as some form of coping mechanism for people who have PTSD, and may play a role in helping them eliminate stress and other types of anxiety. It doesn't mean trichotillomania should be encouraged as a coping mechanism, though.

Interestingly enough, other studies also found that trichotillomania is related to different types of emotional avoidance. In other words, people use the behaviors associated with trichotillomania to 'stifle' negative emotions that form due to conditions like PTSD or other depressive conditions.

Of course, the negative effects of having

trichotillomania play a role in worsening how people handle their PTSD (and other depressive disorders), making it imperative for them to seek treatment for both instead of 'self-medicating.'

Though, the way trichotillomania works is a little tricky. A lot of people who already know about trichotillomania know that it's the condition that makes people compulsively yank and/or pick out their hair. Many resources, however, class trichotillomania in a different way, generally based on its inherent characteristics.

Classifying Trichotillomania

Many resources define trichotillomania as a type of 'self induced and/or recurrent source of hair loss.' The defining characteristic is its tendancy to make people feel an impending or blossoming urgency to pick or yank out their hair before they partake in the act itself.

Some sources point to the fact that people who have trichotillomania don't actually feel the impending and/or blossoming urgency to pick their hair. For those people, their compulsive hair yanking behaviors tend to be 'automatic,' as in they unconsciously tug or yank their hair, as if it's a completely natural action for them to do.

Conscious or deliberate hair picking would best describe the impending sense of urgency people feel before they pick their hair. These people generally pluck or yank out their hair to feel the resultant sensations from tearing out their hair. In many cases, these sensations make them feel relief, particularly if they're tearing their hair out of stress or anxiety.

Automatic, unconscious. Deliberate, conscious. Both are concepts of trichotillomania that we'll review in more detail later in this book. Though, before we move to the next section, there's something else we need to see.

Obsessive-compulsive disorder—does it sounds familiar? If it does, you probably know it from popular culture. Obsessive compulsive disorder is much more than what pop culture makes of it. In fact, it's a debilitating disorder for many people. Trichotillomania and OCD actually share a lot of similar traits, since they're both a type of habit disorder. Nowadays, they're considered so closely related that trichotillomania is often a resultant disorder from developing obsessive-compulsive disorder.

Later in this book, we'll be exploring more about trichotillomania as an impulse control disorder and a form of habit disorder. Now, let's move to the next section.

The Qualifications Of Trichotillomania

We know that trichotillomania is a type of impulsive hair pulling. But, have you wondered what really makes trichotillomania, trichotillomania?

According to the *Diagnostic and Statistical Manual,* sanctioned by the American Psychiatric Association (revision DSM-IV), trichotillomania is defined under 5 specific criteria, which are used to determine a diagnosis in patients:

- Repetitive hair picking or yanking, resulting in a considerable or noticeable level of hair loss.
- Tense feelings before the tearing starts or when attempting to resist the need to tear out their hair.
- Distinct feelings of satisfaction or relief when yanking hair or after yanking hair.
- Ruling out any other medical and/or psychiatric problems that might cause those particular symptoms.
- Any disruption in one or several areas in the life of the affected person.

The aforementioned criteria are also used by the World Health Organization to determine a proper diagnosis for trichotillomania. Sometimes, people are diagnosed with trichotillomania, even when all five criteria aren't present in their behaviors. Of course, the diagnosis depends on how the person exhibits behaviors similar to trichotillomania.

Others might be ashamed to reveal they might have problems coping with trichotillomania. Many patients attempt to hide or disguise their symptoms, due to feelings of shame and embarrassment. Due to the condition of this disorder, it's difficult to tell whether someone suffers from it or not. In most cases, a person can hide their symptoms by:

Disguising their hair, usually by wearing hats, wigs or other hair-pieces.
Performing the behaviors out of sight of others, especially if focused behaviors.

Finding ways to get out of social or other types of situations, in order to engage in trichotillomania-related behaviors.

Though, when you think about it, many of these avoidance-related behaviors might indicate there's something wrong with the person suffering from trichotillomania. Of course, this leads to denial by the persons themselves, until they're able to get assistance for fighting some of the more persistent symptoms of trichotillomania.

Unveiling Trichotillomania

When we talk about unveiling trichotillomania, we mean taking a closer look at how the condition 'ticks,' as they say. As a compulsive disorder, trichotillomania can be, well, tricky to characterize. Though, like many disorders of its ilk, there are key characteristics that help people find some type of definition for the condition itself.

Part of finding out the 'true' face of trichotillomania involves taking a closer look at what causes the condition. Finding the exact cause, however, might be trickier than you think.

Trichotillomania... And Its Complications

As mentioned in previous sections, trichotillomania doesn't have a clear or known exact cause. What people do know is that trichotillomania tends to emerge from a combination of both environmental and genetic factors. Some medical experts have found that the natural brain chemicals, dopamine and serotonin, might play a role in the onset of trichotillomania.

Trichotillomania is also known to cause complications. Some of these complications may reveal the cause behind the condition itself. Many of the following conditions develop as a result of trichotillomania, though some people might not assume they result from trichotillomania, since they're related to symptoms of other (and often similar) conditions.

- **Hair and skin damage** – Constant hair pulling or tearing causes abrasions and other damage to the scalp, including infections resulting from the lacerations there. It also affects the specific areas where the hair loss occurs, sometimes affecting hair growth, as well.
- **Hairballs** – People who eat their hair after tearing it out may develop what's known as a *trichobezoar* or large matted hairball in their digestive tract. If not treated, this hairball can cause weight loss, intestinal obstruction, vomiting and, in rare cases, death.
- **Emotional distress** – People who have trichotillomania notably feel ashamed, embarrassed and/or humiliated because of their disorder. It causes them to develop low self-esteem, anxiety and depression, especially if they feel they can't control their condition.
- **Social problems** – people who experience trichotillomania may avoid social activities and other opportunities. They might also wear wigs, style their hair to hide bald patches and/or wear false eyelashes.

Some even avoid interacting with other people out of fear of them discovering their condition.

Even though these symptoms are commonly associated with trichotillomania, they're also associated with other similar disorders. Some facets of obsessive-compulsive disorder, as an example, may cause people to develop behaviors related to trichotillomania. So, even though a person may yank out their hair, it doesn't necessarily mean they have trichotillomania.

The severity of how they tear out their hair, however, determines whether they might have trichotillomania. In fact, the condition is mainly defined by severe hair pulling, since it happens gradually and enough to cause the sufferer distress on a regular basis.

Trichotillomania... And Its Diagnosis

Trichotillomania isn't only diagnosed based on a few symptoms. As mentioned in a previous section, trichotillomania is diagnosed based on a set of criteria as established by the *Diagnostic and Statistical Manual of Mental Disorders*. This helps medical and mental health providers accurately diagnose the condition of their patient in order to determine the best possible treatment options.

When it comes to children, any potential symptoms of trichotillomania are assessed over a period spanning several months at a time. This generally helps doctors make sure their diagnosis of trichotillomania is correct. This system is necessary to confirm whether a child's hair picking or yanking is habitual or the type of hair picking behaviors associated with trichotillomania.

Children often develop a short-term hair pulling habit, so some parents may mistake that for some form of a compulsive disorder. That's why many children need several evaluations before their doctor can confidently confirm the child has trichotillomania.

Young adults and adults are evaluated a little differently since their symptoms often last for longer periods. Before assigning a diagnosis, the doctor rules out any other possible cause for their symptoms. Hair picking or yanking is associated with other disorders, so those particular disorders have to be ruled out before the patient gets a diagnosis of trichotillomania.

People who suspect they might have trichotillomania should have their doctor evaluate them to determine whether they have the condition. Doctors usually perform a complete evaluation to find out more about a patient's experience with the condition. They may:

- Examine how much hair loss the patient has.
- Discuss their hair loss issues and/or have them fill out a questionnaire to learn more about their condition.
- Eliminate other possible causes of hair loss or hair tearing through testing.

The aforementioned 'steps' describe some ways that doctors diagnose trichotillomania in people. In later sections, we'll take a closer look at how doctors actually diagnose trichotillomania.

Until then, let's learn a little more about how trichotillomania affects people on a physical, mental and personal level.

Chapter 2: How Trichotillomania Affects People

As mentioned in our last chapter, the causes and origins of trichotillomania in people are largely unknown. Many resources have attempted to find some sort of cause behind trichotillomania, though it's largely attributed to several factors based on genetics, environmental factors or a combination of both.

Some of those factors comprise the most prevalent explanations for trichotillomania as a disorder. The following explanations have been used as clarifications when examining the onset and eventual management of the disorder:

As a coping mechanism for anxiety or other stressful events – Some people may use trichotillomania as a way to cope with anxiety or other stress-inducing events. The condition may make them use the sensations from hair tearing or picking as a 'coping mechanism.'

As a benign (harmless) habit developed from a sensory event or another type of behavior event – Hair picking or yanking can originate from a harmless habit. It usually develops into conditions like trichotillomania when the habit becomes associated with negative emotions and the positive feelings induced by the disordered behaviors.

As a behavior that occurs in conjunction with another habitual behavior, such as thumb sucking in young children – Behaviors associated with trichotillomania usually start at a young age, which often include hair tugging or yanking. Hair yanking, thumb sucking and other repetitive behaviors are typical for many young children. If they don't cease as behaviors, they may develop into conditions like trichotillomania.

As an indicator of deficiencies, such as serotonin deficiency, where they brain may lack proper levels of the neurotransmitter serotonin – Research indicates that a deficiency of serotonin may lead to the development of trichotillomania. The connection was theorized from the discovery of treating selected trichotillomania patients with selective serotonin reuptake inhibitors (SSRIs).

As an indicator of structural brain abnormalities or an abnormal brain metabolism – The use of magnetic resonance imaging, otherwise known as MRIs, found that some people who have trichotillomania were found to have abnormalities of the lenticulate.

As an indicator of genetic susceptibility, in regards to how people may develop trichotillomania if

another relative developed the condition –
Evidence where people have genetic susceptibility to
trichotillomania have been discovered, especially for
people who have had first degree relatives
experience trichotillomania.

**Psychological factors, including sensory
stimulation, emotional regulation and stress
reduction** – These particular factors have been used
to explain how trichotillomania develops in children.

Disordered reward processing – Some studies have
found that trichotillomania may represent 'a type of
disordered altered reward processing in the nervous
system.'

Neurodegenerating disease associations – Some
instances of trichotillomania have a possible
association with symptoms of neurodegenerating
diseases, including dementia and Parkinson's
disease, in older people.

All these explanations comprise some of the most notable
explanations for how trichotillomania may develop in
many people. Although they serve well as explanations,
they're not as concrete as explanations for the disorder as
some would expect.

Remember: trichotillomania is hard to define, especially
when a lot of people experience it in different ways. In fact,

let's take a closer look at how people experience trichotillomania.

In the previous chapter, we focused a lot on the technical aspects of trichotillomania, but we didn't really cover how trichotillomania really affects your life. And, this disorder affects people in various ways.

Trichotillomania isn't actually as much of a harmful behavior as it's one that can quickly deteriorate one's life. Trichotillomania manifests in conjunction with other psychological conditions, though it's best known as an individual body focused repetitive behavior.

That repetitive behavior often leads to a person picking or pulling out their hair on a regular basis. Sometimes, this behavior manifests as yanking or picking hair from dolls or fibrous materials like clothes or blankets.

Trichotillomania is either:

- **Focused behaviors**, where people tear out their hair intentionally for the purpose of relieving stress or tension. As mentioned in the last chapter, this behavior is also known as conscious behavior, where people deliberately perform an action to get a result.
- **Automatic behaviors**, where people yank out their hair when they don't realize they're doing it. This usually happens when people reflexively tug their hair as a coping mechanism. These behaviors are

also known as unconscious behaviors, since they're usually performed without the intention of doing it.

Many people who experience trichotillomania actually perform both types of behaviors, generally depending on the situation and their mood. Some may even develop situational triggers that provoke the behaviors leading to hair yanking or tearing.

No matter how it happens, the loss of hair causes people to experience negative feelings, directly affecting their self-esteem. When you look at it that way, trichotillomania can play a large role in how you conduct your life.

The Cosmetic Impact Of Trichotillomania

Trichotillomania undoubtedly has a cosmetic impact on people who suffer from the condition. The act of hair tearing causes a person to yank out a little or a significant amount of hair from their scalp. And, when people lose a significant amount of hair from their scalp, it (at least to them) negatively impacts their physical appearance.

→ Trichotillomania and hair loss

Hair loss is something people deal with on a daily basis. Most people regularly shed their hair, though some people face hair loss due to factors beyond their control. For men, hair loss is more or less a genetic occurrence that happens to some men as they age. Most women deal with hair loss as a result of stress or other hormonal changes to their body.

Sometimes, hair loss is attributed to other factors like conditions or diseases that affect the entire body. When you look at those diseases or conditions, you'll see that hair loss is a common symptom of various conditions and diseases. For any instance where a person temporarily or permanently loses their hair, medical professionals use the term known as alopecia, which refers to hair loss.

Since hair is rather important to how people perceive their looks in modern society, many people feel distressed by the prospect of losing their hair. It's that reason why hair loss, in general, is considered a 'bad thing' to people everywhere.

According to medical resources, most men and women experience hair loss due to genetics. Most accounts of baldness or alopecia (at least 95 percent) happen due to genetic factors. The remaining 5 percent is attributed to other factors, including the aforementioned hormonal changes, diet changes, stress, illness or medications. Vitamins and/or mineral supplements can cause hair loss, in addition to medications that treat various medical conditions like high blood pressure. Special treatments, such as chemotherapy, also cause hair loss in patients.

Hair loss being a common side effect of using

medications or special medical treatments doesn't stop people from utilizing those resources. It doesn't, however, stop them from feeling defeated by the prospect of hair loss.

People, especially women, feel defeated by hair loss for various reasons, though most of those reasons affect how a man or woman perceives themselves. In other words, hair loss directly 'attacks' the self-esteem of men and women, though in different ways.

Women with trichotillomania might feel powerless over their hair loss, especially since they're in 'control' of how often they lose hair. Hair loss is said to inflict a significant psychological impact on women. Hair, in general, is considered a large part of a woman's look in modern society, to the point where shorter (or bald) hairstyles aren't as popular as long hairstyles.

When women lose their hair, they feel as if they're losing their sense of style and their sense of security in being perceived by other people. Coupled with a trichotillomania diagnosis, a woman may feel like she can't control her hair loss and, ultimately, can't control her trichotillomania.

Men with trichotillomania might feel the same about their hair loss—not having any control over how often they lose hair. While societal expectations don't affect men as much as women, when it comes to hair loss, they do deal with societal expectations in that regard. That's why men with trichotillomania may experience feelings of anxiety or become depressed if they feel they can't control how often they tear out their hair. A lot of men already experience hair thinning as they get older. Men with trichotillomania might feel powerless over controlling how often their hair loss occurs, especially if they can't control how often they yank out their hair.

As you can see, both men and women suffer greatly when it comes to experiencing hair loss. Coupled with trichotillomania, hair loss can fast become a potentially emotionally devastating experience if not treated.

So, how does hair yanking or picking out hairs negatively impact a person's cosmetic appearance? To start, hair yanking is an action that actively removes hair from a person's scalp, reducing the number of visible hairs on their scalp.

When that happens, the person starts developing a number of balding spots. Sometimes, these balding spots cluster together and form entire stretches of balding scalp. People who have severe instances of trichotillomania tend to pick and tear out their hair until they develop these noticeable balding spots. Yanking out hair from thinning areas is also common in people who have trichotillomania.

Of course, the presence of balding spots on the scalp makes people feel embarrassed, ashamed or even depressed. As mentioned in a previous section, hair is one part of a person's complete 'look.' In other words, people in today's society expect others to have hair. People who experience hair loss (or those without hair) sometimes feel the pressure of having to have a 'full head of hair' to be a well-meaning member of society.

Can you imagine how people who have trichotillomania feel? Not only do trichotillomania sufferers experience hair loss, but also they experience hair loss that they can't control themselves. That easily makes people with the disorder feel like they can't control their lives, since they can't control their hair loss.

To go more into detail about that, many who have trichotillomania feel like their behaviors (hair pulling and, sometimes, hair eating) are shameful behaviors to partake in. And, the more they beat themselves up over those behaviors, the more they beat on their self-esteem. That's why many who have trichotillomania find dealing with the condition difficult at first.

Sometimes, the hair picking resulting from trichotillomania results in physical ailments. Some people tear out their hair so much that it causes bleeding on their scalp. The lacerations on their scalp then gain an increased risk of infection if not cared for properly.

One of the biggest medical concerns of trichotillomania involves people who eat their hair. People who feel a compulsion to swallow their hair sometimes experience gastrointestinal distress. In rare cases, they develop obstructions within their intestinal system, which might cause them to need surgery to have the blockage removed. While the physical effects of trichotillomania are relatively uncommon, they're a very real concern for people who have trichotillomania.

According to studies regarding trichotillomania, people who have 'no history of psychological disorders (of different ages and genders) were shown to have trichotillomania significantly impact many aspects of their life, including their ability to function socially.'

A similar study also showed that people who suffered from trichotillomania were 'more likely to experience periods of depression.' They also were shown to have more trouble dealing with certain aspects of daily life, including that of physical health, grooming, recreation, work, social interaction and managing their own self-esteem.

Learning how trichotillomania affects people is probably one of the biggest hurdles to uncovering how to demystify, treat and manage the disease. That's the reason so many studies and research trials exist, to see how hair loss alone affects people, in addition to those who exclusively deal with managing trichotillomania.

In order to take a closer look at how trichotillomania affects people, we need to uncover the signs, symptoms and causes of trichotillomania. Even though we've reviewed those aspects of trichotillomania in previous sections, it's now time to take a closer look at them.

The Signs, Symptoms And Causes Of Trichotillomania

People who have trichotillomania compulsively yank out their hair. Some people even consume their torn out hairs. As an impulse control disorder, various reasons exist for why people develop trichotillomania. Learning how those reasons originate involves taking a closer look at how trichotillomania 'works.'

The Signs Of Trichotillomania

People who have different types of disorders often exhibit different signs of having the disorder in question. Although outside parties may detect something 'off' about the person, the person experiencing the disorder often doesn't feel that there's anything wrong. That reason alone is a big reason why disorders like trichotillomania go untreated.

The signs of trichotillomania manifest gradually, usually after childhood. They usually appear after childhood, due to the fact that younger children often stop hair yanking or tugging after engaging in the activity for certain periods of time. By the time they reach adolescence, people with some form of trichotillomania already show signs of having the disorder.

In most cases, people who have trichotillomania exhibit signs of hair pulling, either through the presence of balding spots on their scalp or signs of significant hair shedding. Since the most prevalent place people yank out hairs is from the scalp, people who have trichotillomania typically show signs of having the condition there at first.

The Symptoms Of Trichotillomania

As mentioned in the previous chapter, the *APA Diagnostic and Statistical Manual* criteria (revision DSM-IV) for diagnosing a person with trichotillomania is:

> → Repetitive hair pulling, resulting in a considerable or noticeable level of hair loss.
> → Tense feelings before the pulling starts or when attempting to resist the urge to pull.
> → Distinct feelings of satisfaction or relief when pulling hair or after pulling hair.
> → Ruling out any other medical and/or psychiatric problems that might cause those particular symptoms.
> → Any disruption in one or several areas in the life of the affected person.

So, looking at that set of criteria again, the main symptom of trichotillomania undoubtedly involves **moderate to severe hair pulling**.

The Case With Hair Pulling And Trichotillomania

Hair pulling is the biggest and most visible symptom of trichotillomania. In fact, it defines the disorder itself. Since there are several places on the body where hair grows, people aren't limited to tearing or yanking out hair in just one place of the body.

Most who have trichotillomania yank their hair directly from their scalp, however others are known to pluck or tug their hair from other places on the body. This includes the arms, the legs, the pubic region and even around the eyes. Some people restrict their hair yanking to one part of the body, while others tug their hair out in multiple places on their body at a time. In most cases, people who have trichotillomania yank out their hair without the intention to cause themselves any harm or pain.

→ Signs of trichotillomania

People who have trichotillomania don't immediately exhibit signs. In most cases, people attempt to hide the fact that they have trichotillomania. Though, doctors have ways to find out if their patient has some form of trichotillomania.

When a person has some form of trichotillomania, they usually have hair of varying lengths, particularly lengths that indicate new hair growth in sporadic areas of their scalp. People who have very short hair and a fair number of broken hairs typically have some form of trichotillomania.

People who have severe cases of trichotillomania have thinning or balding parts of their scalp. They also may have thinning or balding patches on other parts of their body, including their eyebrows, eyelashes or pubic region.

Since people easily find ways to cover up their thinning or balding hair, it's not as easy to see if a person has trichotillomania or not, just by relying on their looks alone.

People who pull out their hair, because of trichotillomania, may experience episodes lasting as short as a few minutes or as long as a few hours. Most episodes take place during periods of relaxation or even stress.

People who have trichotillomania may even have preferences regarding the type of hair they need to yank or pluck out; some people have different colors, textures or qualities they prefer in hair. As mentioned, people who have trichotillomania have hair of differing lengths. We mentioned that they usually have patches of hair with new growth, particularly if their trichotillomania is severe. There are actually quite a few variances in how hair looks on people who have trichotillomania.

Some people have broken hairs with blunt and/or broken ends, while others have hairs broken mid-shaft. Some people have uneven stubble where they've broken hair off at the root. Ultimately, people who yank or tear out their hair leave their hair in an unhealthy state, since their hair remains unkempt and damaged after their hair yanking sessions.

We also mentioned that people pick their hair from different parts of their body, though we didn't exactly mentioned how frequently people pick their hair from certain parts of their body. People who have trichotillomania pick their hair in one or two sites at a time.

The most prevalent site is the scalp, though people are known to pluck the hair of their face, arms, legs, eyebrows and eyelashes. Some of the most prevalent areas where people pluck or tear out hair include the pubic area, underarms, chest and beards (for men). Most adults vary where they tug or yank out hair; children are less likely to tug their hair in other areas besides the scalp itself.

A 'classic' presentation of trichotillomania is known as the 'Friar Tuck' presentation of crown and vertex alopecia. It's called 'Friar Tuck,' since it resembles the hairstyle of the Robin Hood character, Friar Tuck. The hairstyle often depicts hair around the sides of the head and the back of the neck and head, meeting into a crown that lines the entire head.

People who have trichotillomania actually pluck out their hairs one at a time. In most cases, these hair plucking episodes last hours on end. It does, however, go into a remission-like state where people don't have the impulse to yank or tear out their hair for days, weeks, months and even years on end.

People who have trichotillomania often experience the following during their hair plucking rituals:

- Twirling hair off the root or examining the hair's roots
- Oral behaviors, such as running hair across their teeth, biting off the hair root (trichopathy) or eating

their hair (trichophagia)

Many people who have trichotillomania may attempt to control their hair plucking or tugging behaviors in the presence of others or outright perform their ritualistic behaviors in private. That reason alone is a big reason why trichotillomania, as mentioned, goes 'undetected' in people who have it.

Hair plucking or tearing may be attributed to another type of psychological disorder, which is another reason why trichotillomania might not be immediately diagnosed in people who exhibit signs of the condition. When every other possible reason for hair tearing or plucking gets ruled out, people who tear out their hair get a trichotillomania diagnosis.

→ The patterns of trichotillomania

Like with many disorders, people who have trichotillomania exhibit different behaviors that more or less characterize the disorder. When multiple people exhibit those behaviors between cases of trichotillomania, it creates a pattern of similar behaviors.

On an interesting note, there are actually no concrete patterns in people who have trichotillomania, since people who have it tend to yank or tear out hairs from their preferred places. In this case, patterns refer to the similar actions people perform when suffering from a specific disorder.

Medical professionals then use those patterns to form a complete profile of different disorders, just like they did for trichotillomania.

Known patterns of trichotillomania

- Many people tear hair away from the scalp, while others pluck hairs from areas of their face, their pubic region, their legs and their arms.

- About half of people afflicted with trichotillomania pluck hair using tweezers during some of their episodes.

- More than half of people who have trichotillomania are known to specifically target tugging out hairs with a certain texture, feel or look, particularly hairs that are thick or coarse.

- People who have the condition often feel compelled to play with and/or stroke the hair they tugged out. Some people check the hair's root to ensure it completely came out when tugged.

- Some people bite off the root of their plucked out hairs. In a study regarding the subject, 1/3 of patients were found to have engaged in root biting. About 20 percent were found to have eaten the entire hair.

Many of the patterns emerging from how people handle their cases of trichotillomania more or less indicate common trends with the disorder. By observing these patterns, people who have trichotillomania and medical providers learn more about how to manage the disorder.

Hair pulling, as a concept, is pretty simple to understand. People yank and tug out their hairs from their hair follicles. How people engage in hair yanking or tugging, however, is where the compulsive behavior can get rather complex.

How People Engage In Hair Pulling

People who have trichotillomania tug out their hair in different ways. Therefore, there are no real 'rules' or 'guidelines' determining a concrete set of behaviors for people who have trichotillomania to exhibit.

So, there are many instances where people feel compelled to tug out (and, sometimes, consume) their hair. The following are some examples showing how people who have trichotillomania handle hair yanking or tearing:

- Some people tear out their hair when they feel stressed and/or anxious.
- Some people pluck out their hair when they feel

relaxed and/or calm.

- Some people tug out their hair during mundane activities, such as watching television or resting.
- Some people tug out their hair when they are about to fall asleep or are asleep. Environmental factors are actually known to play some role in influencing how trichotillomania is affected by sleep. Sleep-induced 'automatic' trichotillomania is known as sleep-isolated trichotillomania.
- Some people yank out their hair as a means of coping with other psychological disorders.

People typically develop trichotillomania at a young age, but how it progresses happens in different ways. In most cases, people develop the disorder out of a means to cope with stressful life events. Others develop trichotillomania after observing the behavior or accidentally engaging in said behaviors.

In other words, the common triggers for trichotillomania are more or less unique triggers, otherwise triggers that only apply to the person who experiences trichotillomania.

What Hair Pulling Feels Like

People who have trichotillomania look at the condition in a different perspective than people who don't. In fact, trichotillomania looks different and, in most cases, strange to people who don't have the condition. They see their loved ones inexplicably tugging out their hair without any rhyme or reason. Since they don't know what thoughts or emotions occur when the loved one pulls out his/her hair, they can't really understand why they engage in those behaviors.

So, you're probably wondering what trichotillomania feels like for people who have the condition. Trichotillomania manifests in people in different ways, and we've already covered that in previous sections. Though, the types of behaviors that people do experience with trichotillomania have some sort of pattern.

People who have trichotillomania have reported feeling:

- An overwhelming compulsion to tug out their hairs. Sometimes, this manifests as an overwhelming sense of anxiety or need to tug out their hair. When they tear out their hair, they immediately feel relieved or relaxed.
- An overwhelming surge of guilt. Many people who have trichotillomania experience a guilt cycle. When they feel guilty for yanking or tearing out their hair, they often repeat those compulsive behaviors, more or less trapping themselves in a cycle of tearing out their hair.

The need to tug out hair and the guilt occurring after it describes two of the most prevalent behaviors in trichotillomania. While it might seem difficult to break this cycle, treatment and behavior management can help people break even the toughest cases of trichotillomania.

Determining A Trichotillomania Diagnosis

The best way to learn if you or a loved one has trichotillomania is seeking assistance from a health care provider. Doctors have the tools needed to rule out any instances of hair pulling unrelated to trichotillomania.

Many dermatological and other medical conditions provoke hair tearing or yanking, making it difficult to immediately assume that someone may have trichotillomania. That's the main reason why people who have trichotillomania receive full physical examinations to find other sources of the issue. If hair pulling is the only symptom that dominates any other symptoms, the person engaging in any hair tearing or yanking behaviors likely only has trichotillomania.

Before doctors rule trichotillomania as their sole condition, people who exhibit symptoms also need a psychological evaluation. This helps doctors learn if the hair tearing or yanking is a symptom of a psychological disorder, typically an underlying one. One of the biggest goals of the evaluation process is finding out if there are any underlying psychological issues, so they can immediately be treated. In some cases, patients are asked about their daily life, their past and their emotions to provide doctors with further information about their medical condition.

→ Why people with trichotillomania pull out their hair

People who have trichotillomania tug out their hair for various reasons. Depending on the person's need and urges, their reasons for tearing out their hair will be different from other people.

Some people actually develop trichotillomania out of a need to regulate their moods. Many patients have actually reported that tugging out hair has a significant effect on the way they feel.

Some people feel energized and/or motivated (when fatigued or bored) after they tug out their hair. Other people feel the opposite effect: tearing or yanking out their hair usually makes them feel calm and relaxed during periods of tension and/or stress.

Hair tearing or yanking, for these patients, also distracts them from negative emotions, and plays a role in eliminating negative feelings altogether.

Other people pluck out their hair for cosmetic reasons. They may feel they need to make their eyelashes, eyebrows or other parts of their body look more symmetric. Many people, in fact, start plucking their hairs out to get rid of unsightly and/or irregular hairs. Hairs that are darker, longer, thicker or coarser than other hairs are frequent targets. Of course, many people compulsively pluck out their gray hairs.

Some instances of hair tearing or yanking are done to feel a sensation that's unique to the person doing the action. Some people who have trichotillomania interpret this feeling as a 'tingling' sensation, while other feel an itching sensation.

There are people that utilize their trichotillomania as a coping mechanism, especially if they have another psychological condition. It also helps people cope with feelings of sadness, anxiety, frustration or outright boredom. Many people rely on hair tearing or yanking until they find another and, often, healthier coping mechanism. Finding healthier coping mechanisms is the best way to help people learn how to manage their trichotillomania.

Even though trichotillomania isn't harmful in nature, people who have the condition still need treatment to resolve the condition's inherent problems. Trichotillomania causes psychological harm and, in some cases, physical harm to people who experience the disorder. It's that reason why people need to seek treatment.

Before we look into the various treatment options of trichotillomania, let's look at the causes of the disorder.

The Causes Of Trichotillomania

People want to know why they develop trichotillomania, especially if they experience the negative effects of the condition on a regular basis. Some of the questions people ask themselves about trichotillomania include:

- Why did I develop trichotillomania?
- What caused me to develop trichotillomania?
- Why do people get trichotillomania?
- Why do some people who have trichotillomania in the family start pulling their hair and others don't?

Many of these questions are easily answered by learning more about how trichotillomania develops as a disorder. The problem with that is many doctors haven't determined whether there's a single, concrete cause of trichotillomania.

The Root Of Trichotillomania's Causes

People don't know exactly why trichotillomania develops. Trichotillomania is actually a condition with multiple triggers or causes, many of which are unique to the people experiencing the disorder. That means that no two people experience the same triggers or cause of trichotillomania, since it manifests in different ways.

Of course, many people share similarities in how they develop the disorder, which is how those trichotillomania patterns we talked about develop. We've talked about some of these triggers earlier in the book, but now we're going to talk about them in detail.

Medical researchers haven't yet pinpointed a singular cause for trichotillomania. Trichotillomania has been theorized to develop as the result of several unique factors that might have come together to make the condition develop. Some assume there's no concrete cause of trichotillomania, and instead that the condition is entirely conditional on behalf of the person who experiences it.

Since research is still being conducted about trichotillomania, it remains among many health conditions that medical science can't fully explain.

→ Trichotillomania and a genetic link?

Many people wonder if genetics plays a role in influencing the development of trichotillomania. While the question is a great question to ask, finding the answer is rather tricky.

One of the biggest reasons why it's difficult to attribute genetics as a cause of trichotillomania is that many people hide the fact that they're suffering from it. For this reason, medical researchers and doctors can't get accurate information from patients, since they're not telling them all the information they need to know in order to form a conclusion on whether genetics really does play a role in development.

Despite the lack of information, there has been research conducted about the link between genetics and trichotillomania. While those particular studies suggest there's no specific gene that 'triggers' the condition, there is a genetic link for many individuals.

That genetic link more or less creates a genetic predisposition, otherwise an increased likelihood, that certain patients who 'meet the criteria' may develop trichotillomania.

Research about trichotillomania and its possible genetic links is still underway today. What many resources have found so far, however, indicate there's a combination of genetic factors that may influence the development of trichotillomania.

So, what causes trichotillomania? As mentioned, trichotillomania doesn't have a concrete cause. There are, however, several factors that support theories relating to the 'true cause' of trichotillomania.

The Environmental Factors Of Trichotillomania

Some resources assume trichotillomania is caused by specific environmental factors.

It's believed that trichotillomania and hair tearing or

yanking behaviors start during certain periods of a person's life, particularly during periods of intense distress or emotional crises. When this happens, the person feels a near uncontrollable desire to tear out their hair, an action that manifests as a compulsion.

Some people start plucking for cosmetic reasons, meaning they could just pluck out their hair to correct something about its overall appearance. When a person starts associating the positive feelings they get from hair tearing or yanking with the action itself, it might cause them to develop trichotillomania. Hair tearing or yanking is one of many actions that harbor some type of a therapeutic effect for people experiencing emotional distress or even boredom.

The positive aspect of that particular behavior is one of the reasons why it's considered an addictive behavior. In fact, some doctors believe trichotillomania is an addictive behavior because of that. When hair tearing or yanking becomes associated with positive reinforcement, it becomes harder for the person performing the action to stop it. Hair tearing or yanking, at that point, is a coping mechanism that makes them feel better, especially if they're feeling negative emotions.

People who have trichotillomania tend to pull out their hair when their anxiety builds to an irresistible point, and they feel they have no choice but to tug out their hair to make themselves feel better. After they rip out their hair, they feel a sense of relief from all of those negative emotions. Due to the positive feelings they feel after tearing or yanking out their hair, typically feelings of relief or elation, it gets harder to actually stop engaging in that compulsive action.

Naturally over time, people who have trichotillomania do develop feelings of guilt and shame, causing their self-esteem to take a large hit. But, when they tug out their hair, those feelings go away again. That's how trichotillomania becomes a cycle for people who suffer from the disorder. Each time they want to break away from the disorder, they get pulled right back in after repeatedly performing the compulsive action.

Environmental factors, such as emotional distress, play a role as one potential cause of trichotillomania. It's not the only cause, however.

The Case With Trichotillomania As A Habit Disorder

Is trichotillomania a habit disorder? That's one common theory people have about the true cause of trichotillomania. The theory supports the idea that trichotillomania isn't a behavior disorder, because it harbors traits making it more of a habit disorder.

The main idea behind this theory is hair yanking more or less turns into an 'ingrained habit' where the brain's basal ganglia (the part of the brain influencing habit formation) adapts to the compulsive behavior and expects that behavior. In this theory, another part of the brain, the frontal lobes, don't perform their job of rejecting or suppressing these habits, instead making the habit remain ingrained.

Some sources think trichotillomania as a habit disorder makes more sense than it being a behavioral disorder. A lot of it has to do with how the brain itself operates.

The brain's neurotransmitters carry messages throughout the brain and the rest of the body, regulating our behaviors, movements and impulses. If the brain's neurotransmitters contract some type of disorder, they trigger repetitive and compulsive behaviors, which is how trichotillomania and other related conditions likely form.

Trichotillomania is said to work much like other habit disorders. That's another reason why some resources support trichotillomania as a habit disorder. It's also considered similar to obsessive-compulsive disorder, in the sense that it makes people exhibit the same symptoms. Some medications used to treat OCD were even found to subside symptoms from trichotillomania, as well.

The fact that trichotillomania behaviors encompass all other behaviors largely supports its potential status as a habit disorder. When people feel a compulsion to tug out their hair, they often can't think of anything else but committing to that particular action.

They can't stop their desire to tug out their hair until they actually perform the action, and it's the only action that will make their need to tear out their hair go away. Though, since the desire to tug out hair is a compulsion, the trichotillomania is known to come back just as fast as the previous behaviors happened. The body also becomes expectant of the relief provided by the hair tearing or yanking, making it even harder for people to stop yanking out their hair.

As you can see, trichotillomania does have some evidence supporting it as a habit disorder. Though, until there's concrete research regarding the matter, the evidence only serves as some proof supporting that theory.

The Case With Trichotillomania As An Overlapping Symptom

This theory supports trichotillomania as a symptom of an overlapping disorder or an overlapping disorder itself. The interesting thing about this theory is that it's actually a widely believed theory.

Many doctors believe trichotillomania manifests as a symptom of another disorder. They also believe it manifests as a coping mechanism to help treat and/or manage a secondary condition. Unlike the other theories we've talked about, this particular theory actually has a significant amount of evidence supporting it.

→ Trichotillomania as a coping mechanism?

A coping mechanism is an adaptation to environmental stress that people start performing to help them regain control over their disordered behaviors. Coping mechanisms also serve as a way to give people psychological comfort over having to deal with environmental-based stress or other negative factors.

The nature of hair tearing or yanking is seen as a coping mechanism. Hair tugging can be considered one of the many spontaneous actions people do when they're under a lot of stress. Vigorously scratching the head, pacing back and forth and fingernail biting are all actions considered similar to hair tearing or yanking, since people typically perform them when they're under a lot of stress.

When it comes to hair tearing or yanking, a lot of people do this to cope with stress, anxiety or a myriad of negative emotions. Many theories support trichotillomania developing as a response to stress. People who yank out their hair for the first time may get a sense of relief, and may continue to do it again as a stress reliever. By then, their brain is already used to the response that hair tearing or yanking invokes, which is why they tend to repeat the action over and over again.

So, when people use hair yanking as a coping mechanism, their bodies naturally adjust to the feelings hair tearing produces, and that's what causes them to develop trichotillomania once the hair yanking becomes severe.

For that reason, trichotillomania can be considered a coping mechanism.

People who have trichotillomania often start tearing their hair out of a response to their emotions. When they feel nervous, out of control or sad, they start pulling out their hair. The fact that many doctors and medical researchers have performed studies regarding trichotillomania's connection with other mental disorders supports the apparent connection between hair tugging and emotional relief.

Anxiety, depression and obsessive-compulsive disorder in adults and children was found to have some kind of link with trichotillomania. Research regarding that connection found that people who have those particular diagnoses were more likely to engage in hair tearing or yanking. Although a connection was found there, it's unclear whether those particular disorders played a role in causing the development trichotillomania. In most cases, hair yanking is a coping mechanism for people who have those particular disorders.

Post-traumatic stress disorder is another disorder that overlaps with trichotillomania in some way. Research again showed that a large percentage of trichotillomania cases were found to have developed as a response to prolonged instances of stress.

Although there's a very strong case for trichotillomania occurring as a symptom of an overlapping disorder, there's still no concrete cause of trichotillomania's development.

→ Trichotillomania and endorphins

Trichotillomania might be an 'effective' coping tool

for people for one reason: it causes the body to release endorphins, which help influence the positive feelings that eliminate stress and anxiety. It's said that endorphins release during the hair tearing or yanking action; the resultant pain from the yanking is what triggers it.

Endorphins release when our bodies feel pain, and these endorphins actually act as 'opiates' in our systems that help curb the pain. When people discover the endorphin-induced feelings that their hair yanking creates, they start to develop an addiction to that compulsive action, since the very action itself helps release those endorphins.

So, when you look at it that way, hair tearing or yanking releases endorphins and the presence of endorphins helps relieve the emotional pain some people have. That's a possible reason why people who have trichotillomania keep tearing out their hair.

Even though we're trying to find a true cause behind trichotillomania, it doesn't mean we can't rule certain factors as a potential 'origin point' for the disorder. In this case, the cause of trichotillomania in individual people is solely ruled by factors specific to them.

That alone is a good reason why trichotillomania is

diagnosed in the first place. As for a universal cause, finding out the truth behind that will take some much needed time.

Chapter 3: All About The Treatments Of Trichotillomania

In this book, we've talked about most aspects of trichotillomania, including its signs, symptoms and potential causes. Now, we're ready to take a closer look at the treatments used to heal and manage trichotillomania.

Treating Trichotillomania: How Severe Is Your Trichotillomania?

Before finding an appropriate treatment for trichotillomania, it's important for people to learn more about the severity level of their disorder. After all, people who have a milder case of trichotillomania will need different treatment than people who have severe trichotillomania.

Much like other health conditions, trichotillomania has a spectrum that determines the severity of the condition. Severity, in this case, refers to the frequency and emotional impact of trichotillomania in people. Let's take a closer look at trichotillomania's degrees of severity in people who have the condition.

Temporary trichotillomania

Temporary trichotillomania is perhaps the mildest form of the condition, since it typically lasts for a short amount of time.

In most cases, babies and very young children get this form. Teenagers and adults can also develop this form of trichotillomania, though it's more common in younger children.

Patients with this form of the disorder experience a mostly subconscious form of this condition. The hair tugging action is typically performed in response to stress or other negative emotions. Although younger children typically have this form, little is understood about why they develop trichotillomania in this way.

Medical experts do believe, however, that trichotillomania occurs in children for similar reasons to older people (as a response to stress).

Patients with this form of trichotillomania may have their disorder go unnoticed. Some don't even express concern over their trichotillomania if it's this mild. These cases typically last as long as a few days, a few weeks or a few months. If it lasts for years, it happens on an irregular basis.

Even though it's one of the least worrisome forms of trichotillomania, people do seek treatment for it if they feel it disturbs some aspects of their life.

Mild trichotillomania

This mild to moderate form of the condition occurs on a frequent basis, but typically doesn't lean to severe hair loss and/or medical complications.

Mild trichotillomania typically occurs during extreme periods of stress or emotional distress. Sometimes, people engage in this form of trichotillomania when their emotions become too overwhelming. Also, the irresistible impulse to yank out their hair doesn't affect them as often, only appearing on occasions where they'd be provoked into exhibiting that behavior.

People who have milder trichotillomania manage to avoid engaging in its associated behaviors by delegating their attention to other activities. This form of procrastination helps people prevent themselves from engaging in the behavior, causing their hair yanking urges to subside.

They also don't feel the same feelings of distress or panic that people who have severe trichotillomania feel when they tug their hair. Instead, those feelings rarely develop in them and don't last for a long time.

People who have mild trichotillomania rarely show the same cosmetic symptoms as people who have severe cases. Their hair rarely shows any signs of bald spots or thinning, making it easier for them to 'hide' any signs of having trichotillomania in the first place. If they engage in heavier instances of hair tearing or yanking, there might be some signs, though they're generally unnoticeable.

Milder forms of trichotillomania also don't give people any medical complications. This form of trichotillomania rarely ever causes a person to start biting, chewing or swallowing their plucked hairs.

Severe trichotillomania

People who have severe trichotillomania experience some of the more acute symptoms of the condition. The symptoms are often much more pronounced than symptoms associated with milder forms of trichotillomania.

Severe trichotillomania makes people hold onto the urge of yanking out their hair for longer periods of time. For some people, that feeling never goes away. Even if they try to ignore or procrastinate the compulsion to yank or tear out their hair, the urge often grows too strong for them to successfully ignore.

Resisting the desire to tear out hair actually causes severe emotional distress in people suffering from severe trichotillomania. Due to this, it's incredibly difficult for people who have severe trichotillomania to stop tearing or yanking out their hair. It's even harder for them to find a treatment option that will successfully help them stop.

People who have severe trichotillomania often have several visible spots of balding or thinning hair, in one or several locations, on their scalp. Some people tear out so much of their hair that their scalp becomes near or completely bald. Other people who have severe trichotillomania may have only one or several large areas of thinning or balding hair with some patches of new growth.

When people pluck hair from other areas of the body, it results in near or total hair loss on those parts of the body. Some people lose parts of their eyebrows, while others completely pluck out their eyebrows (one or both). Others partially or completely pluck out their eyelashes and patches of hair on their arms, legs or pelvic region.

Due to what severe trichotillomania does to their hair, many patients who suffer from this form of trichotillomania go to great lengths to restore their outer appearance. Many people typically wear wigs, hats, hairpieces and other items to cover their missing hair.

Some people, who have picked hair from their face, draw on eyebrows, use fake eyelashes or even have their eyebrows tattooed on permanently. Even though covering up the condition sounds rather simple, it often takes a great emotional toll on people who have trichotillomania.

Other forms of severe trichotillomania make people interact with their plucked out hairs. Many play with the hairs they plucked from their head or other parts of their body. Some examine their hairs, bite off the roots or even chew on the hairs themselves. Some people even eat their plucked out hairs, a condition we've reviewed already as trichophagia.

→ Trichotillomania and trichophagia

Trichophagia is best known as a condition where people consume the hairs they plucked from their scalp or other parts of their body, otherwise known as the compulsive eating of hair. This condition often develops in people who already have severe forms of trichotillomania.

It develops because many of these people gain a strong compulsion to eat their hair. While some only eat the root bulbs of their hair, others eat the entire hair.

Trichophagia is characterized by its ritualized behavior, which often involves the actual consumption of the hair. Many people start their ritual by touching the hair to their lips or by performing another action before eating the hair itself.

Some people think trichophagia is rather innocuous, but it can get dangerous if left untreated. Humans can develop hairballs in their digestive tract if they keep swallowing hairs. When left untreated, balls of hair may form in the stomach, blocking off the intestinal tract from the stomach; in other cases, hair may even get caught within the intestinal tract itself. Although rare, it's a very real concern for people who consume their hair after plucking it out.

Severe trichotillomania is a rarer form of trichotillomania. People that do have severe trichotillomania often need personalized treatment to effectively treat their condition. Since their instance of trichotillomania doesn't respond to simply ignoring the need to tear hair from their scalp or body, people who have trichotillomania have no option but to seek treatment in order to successfully treat the condition.

Ways To Treat Trichotillomania

Although some people might feel powerless over their trichotillomania, there are many ways they can overcome it. Adults, teenagers and young children can use the following treatments, with help from some medical intervention, to find ways to help them overcome trichotillomania in their lives.

Of course, it takes several tries before finding the right treatment or even combinations of treatments to effectively treat trichotillomania. That's why you shouldn't feel too discouraged about trying different treatments until your doctor helps you find the right treatment for you.

Remember that it takes time to find the right treatment. As long as you keep an open mind, you won't have to feel defeated each time you try researching possible treatments for your trichotillomania. Now, let's take a closer look at the many treatment options for trichotillomania.

Trichotillomania And Medications

Like similar conditions, people do use medications to treat trichotillomania. On the other hand, the Food and Drug Administration hasn't actually approved a medication specifically designed for treating trichotillomania. The medications used to treat trichotillomania primarily help control the symptoms of the disorder.

Some doctors recommend antidepressants, which may curb some of the negative feelings that can provoke the hair tearing or yanking behaviors.

Others recommend medications that play a part in adjusting the brain's neurotransmitters, specifically the ones responsible for influencing urges and compulsions. People who have trichotillomania naturally experience different results from taking the aforementioned medications when treating their trichotillomania.

Selective serotonin re-uptake inhibitors (SSRIs)

Selective serotonin re-uptake inhibitors are the most prevalent medications used to treat trichotillomania.

These drugs include Prozac, Celexa and Zoloft, as a part of a class of drugs considered very effective in treating habit disorders like obsessive-compulsive disorder.

Most people who take SSRIs for trichotillomania start on low doses. As they grow used to the medication, they take increased doses. Most of the time, the medications help with controlling their desire to forcibly tug hair from their scalp or body. Of course, there are some side effects, including their tendency to cause children, teens and adults to develop negative behaviors and thoughts.

Clomipramine

This particular drug is a part of an older class of psychiatric medications. It mainly affects two of the brain's neurotransmitters, norepinephrine and serotonin.

Clomipramine has been proven to be effective in treating compulsions, obsessions and bouts of depression in many patients. It's also approved for children to use, something that other drugs used to treat trichotillomania do not. Side effects for this drug are rather mild and tend to include mild weight gain, constipation and, in some cases, twitches or tremors.

Before selecting an appropriate medication for treating trichotillomania, always talk with your doctor and/or psychiatrist about what medication might suit treating your instance of trichotillomania. In most cases, it takes some time to find an appropriate medication.

Trichotillomania, Behavioral Therapy And Psychotherapy

Psychotherapy is the treatment of mental disorders by psychological means, rather than medical means. When used to treat trichotillomania, it can be effective in helping people eventually reverse negative habits associated with the condition.

Habit reversal training is the main type of psychotherapy used to treat trichotillomania. It mainly helps people understand how to recognize situations where they feel an urge to start pulling out their hair. In place of those behaviors, habit reversal training teaches them how to substitute those behaviors for more acceptable behaviors.

Habit reversal training also combines other forms of psychotherapy to create a more 'complete' treatment process. That usually includes:

- **Cognitive therapy** – A form of therapy that helps people challenge and look deeper into beliefs they might have in association with hair yanking.
- **Acceptance/commitment therapy** – This form of therapy helps people learn how to accept their hair tugging urges without acting on them.

Most people use some form of behavioral therapy (or psychotherapy) for treating trichotillomania. In fact, it's considered one of the most effective forms of treatment for trichotillomania today. It's even effective for people older than 16, especially since adults often have a harder time 'unlearning' their hair tearing habits at an older age.

→ The behavioral strategies of trichotillomania

Several types of behavioral strategies exist for treating trichotillomania. Many of them focus on establishing new habits for the patient to latch onto, in order to successfully curb any old habit that might provoke them enough to tug out their hair.

Habit reversal training is a set of procedures best known as increasing awareness of a habit and teaching a competing response to a habit, especially when the desire to vigorously take out hair from their body or scalp occurs. These procedures teach younger and older people how to react to their habit in situations where it occurs and after it occurs. It also involves teaching people how to reduce both stress and anxiety on a regular basis.

Competing reaction training is a form of habit reversal training where children or adults are taught to replace their hair tearing or yanking urges and behavior with a competing behavior that's considered more acceptable in comparison to the aforementioned. They're usually encouraged to practice the alternative behavior on a daily basis, so they eventually repeat that same behavior when their urges resurface.

Self-monitoring involves systematically observing when the behavior occurs, in addition to recording those responses and evaluating solutions to addressing that behavior.

Relaxation training is another form of habit reversal training where children or adults identify the bodily sensations that occur when they feel tense, and then later apply procedures designed to invoke relaxation after they feel tense. This form of training is usually designed for individuals, since people generally have different thresholds for experiencing stress and tension.

Psychotherapy (communication) involves a child or adult talking to a therapist about their problems with trichotillomania, in addition to making use of many techniques to improve their behavioral and psychological problems caused by the disorder. **Cognitive-behavioral therapy** is a common form of psychotherapy.

Hypnosis is a process where a person's (adult or child) physiologic responses are controlled by focusing their attention on specific mental images, mainly for therapeutic purposes. This technique is usually performed to help a person regain control over their behavior, physical well-being or emotions. When hypnotized, the patient is usually more open to following suggestions (provided by a hypnotist) in order to change their behaviors.

How effective is behavior therapy for treating trichotillomania? Let's take a closer look at how behavioral therapy works when used to treat trichotillomania.

Behavioral Therapy And Trichotillomania

Behavioral therapy, also known as cognitive behavioral therapy, is a form of psychotherapy. As a form of psychotherapy, it's considered one of the most effective treatments for trichotillomania in most parts of the world, including North America.

This form of therapy is especially noted for how patients can receive their own 'customized' program in order to get the best results in treating the condition. It's even considered more effective than medication in this respect, since medication is considered trickier to tailor specifically for individuals.

Behavioral therapy helps patients work to change their thought and behavior patterns, especially the ones that trigger the hair tugging in the first place. Whereas medication helps controls the brain's chemical reactions, behavioral therapy helps control and regulate the behaviors and thoughts resulting from those chemical reactions. That's a good reason why the combination of medication and behavioral therapy works to clear people of their trichotillomania issues.

In this section, we're talking about behavioral therapy, so let's keep going.

Cognitive behavioral therapy not only focuses on the behaviors of the person undergoing treatment, but it also focuses on their feelings and thoughts. The entire process revolves around identifying their thoughts, feelings and behavioral patterns in order to find out what provokes their hair yanking urges and behaviors.

When using cognitive behavioral therapy to identify these behaviors, patients eventually start learning how to change their thoughts and behaviors, in addition to their initial reactions to them. From that point, they can eventually learn how to break the hair tearing or pulling cycle and find other ways to cope with their feelings of stress, tension and/or anxiety.

Self-assessment is an important aspect of many cognitive behavioral therapy treatments.

Self-assessment is:

> *an assessment or evaluation of one's self or one's actions and attitudes, including abilities and failings.*

Within the context of trichotillomania treatment, self-assessment helps people examine why they might keep participating in their compulsive behaviors. Many cognitive behavioral therapy treatments ask patients to note what they might feel when they first develop the uncontrollable need to tug or tear out their hair. They're also asked to note how they might feel and how they might react to tearing out their hair.

Self-assessment ultimately helps people see why they perform certain behaviors and feel a certain way while performing those behaviors. Self-assessment, along with other aspects of cognitive behavioral therapy, helps people figure out what comprises their negative thoughts and behavior patterns, so they can find a solution to resolve them.

When those negative thoughts and patterns get identified,

patients can then start working on finding ways to relieve themselves of those particular behaviors.

How Self-Assessment Defines Cognitive Behavioral Therapy

As mentioned, self-assessment plays a large role in cognitive behavioral therapy, and serves as a way for people who have trichotillomania to work with their doctor and identify possible solutions to successfully treat their disorder.

So, how does self-assessment play a role in helping treat trichotillomania? Self-assessment in cognitive behavioral therapy helps people find solutions for treating their issues. Those solutions often come in the form of treatments.

An example of a possible trichotillomania treatment is relying on sensory sensations to help break the hair tearing cycle. That works by introducing another physical feeling before or during the moment when one feels desire to rip or tear hair away from their body or scalp. So, if you feel a tickling or prickling desire to rip out your hair, touching something like a comb or other object might teach you to resist the urge before you reach to rip out your hair.

When you self assess, you can examine when you might make movements to tug out your hair and why you might feel those urges. If you can pinpoint that, it becomes easier to understand how to approach treatment.

Another notable aspect of cognitive behavioral therapy

involves identifying situations where you might develop a strong need to tug out your hair. When you pay closer attention to how your urges might form, you'll be able to see some similarities in how they occur. Usually, you'll be able to identify certain times, places or emotions that may trigger your hair tearing or yanking behaviors.

When you identify your trichotillomania triggers, you'll be able to start finding ways to address and treat those specific triggers. Ultimately, identifying those triggers is another form of self-assessment anyone with trichotillomania can use to their benefit.

The main purpose of using cognitive behavioral therapy to treat trichotillomania is learning to identify negative emotions and thoughts that provoke your trichotillomania urges. Cognitive behavioral therapy teaches people to stay aware and recognize their negative thoughts and emotions, so they can ultimately understand and eventually replace those thoughts with positive thoughts and their corresponding emotions.

Trichotillomania and Dialectical Behavior Therapy

Another form of therapy used to treat trichotillomania is known as dialectical behavior therapy. This form of therapy is actually a type of psychotherapy, developed by University of Washington psychology researcher, Marsha M. Linehan. Dialectical behavior therapy was developed for treating people who have borderline personality disorder and various symptoms of chronic depression.

Dialectical behavior therapy, also known as DBT, is characterized as an approach that helps people boost the regulation of their emotional and cognitive abilities through learning about the triggers that cause them to enter a 'reactive state.' Reactive state, in that context, would be a state where a person may feel compelled to partake in depressive or compulsive behaviors, such as the hair tearing or yanking of trichotillomania.

This form of psychotherapy also helps people learn how to apply their coping skills to the management of their reactive behaviors. In principle, dialectical behavior therapy assumes that every person participating in the therapy are 'doing the best they can to manage their disorder,' but ultimately lack the skills or positive reinforcement to develop a better way to manage their disorder.

Dialectical behavior therapy combines standard techniques for reality testing and emotion regulation found in cognitive behavioral therapy with concepts like distress tolerance, mindful awareness and acceptance. The aforementioned concepts are actually derived from Buddhist meditative practices.

With those conceptual principles in mind, this form of therapy has actually been said to be effective in treating various psychological and physical conditions like traumatic brain injuries, mood disorders and eating disorders. Research about this form of therapy also indicates it's been effective in treating symptoms (and behaviors) from other conditions like spectrum mood disorders. Is dialectical behavior therapy effective in treating trichotillomania, however?

According to research about the subject, it might be. Although it's been used for the treatment of other psychological disorders, it has recently been introduced as a trichotillomania treatment. Dialectical behavior therapy has made great strides in helping people who have other habit disorders to overcome symptoms, so it's only natural that it can be an effective treatment for managing (and eventually overcoming) hair tearing or yanking.

Dialectical behavior therapy becomes rather interesting when used as a treatment for trichotillomania. As mentioned, this form of therapy employs principles from Buddhist meditative practices: distress tolerance, mindful awareness and acceptance. When used for the treatment of trichotillomania, dialectical behavior therapy allows people who have the condition to examine their experience with the disorder.

Mindfulness is one of the other concepts used in dialectical behavior therapy; it allows patients to become more aware of their thoughts and feelings without having any emotional involvement during their self-examination. It also, as mentioned, focuses on helping people regulate their emotions better. When they're able to achieve this through dialectical behavior therapy, it becomes easier for them to be mindful of their feelings, and eventually avoid succumbing to them.

Succumbing to our emotions is what makes a lot of people fall 'victim' to their repetitive, compulsive behaviors, and it's often what fuels the uncontrollable urges people get when driven to perform those behaviors on a regular basis.

Recognizing those emotions and overcoming them is a big part of dialectical behavioral therapy, especially when it's used for the treatment of trichotillomania.

This form of therapy is also designed to help people improve their problem solving skills, not to mention, their interpersonal effectiveness, otherwise known as their social skills. The way dialectical behavior therapy is designed, people can ultimately learn how to survive their urges and overcome the thought patterns that define their trichotillomania.

Trichotillomania And Hair Replacement Therapy

Hair replacement therapy encompasses everything to do with managing and replacing hair loss. It's especially necessary for people who have trichotillomania, particularly those with severe forms of the disorder.

The extent of hair replacement therapy spans medical, supplemental, pharmaceutical, exercise and fashion related solutions for hair replacement in people who have significant hair loss.

So, what does hair replacement therapy feature? Much of the hair replacement therapy canon includes many of the solutions people use everyday to combat and, eventually, relieve hair loss:

- **Medications** – Although not as successful as other alternative treatments, some medications help people relieve their loss. Some of these medications, such as finasteride, dutasteride and minoxidil are best used in the context of treating male pattern hair loss by preventing further hair loss. Corticosteroids injections help treat hair loss, as do other oral medications designed to help boost hair growth after a few months.
- **Surgery** – Surgery is probably the most prevalent *permanent* option for treating hair loss, especially for men. **Hair transplantation** is a common and permanent solution for treating hair loss; it typically involves a surgeon transplanting healthy hair follicles from the back and sides of the head to a thinning part of the scalp. It usually takes several sessions to rebuild that portion of the scalp, so hair grows back thicker. Other surgical hair loss treatments include **scalp flaps**, **follicle transplants**, **hairline lowering, scalp reductions** and **micro-needling**.
- **Non-surgical** – Non-surgical treatments are undoubtedly the most prevalent way to treat hair loss. They're also the easiest way, too, since they don't involve any invasive surgical procedures. Most people wear wigs, hats, hairpieces and head scarves to mask their hair loss. Some people cut their hair extremely short or even shave their entire head to allow their hair to grow back in evenly. Of course, some people embrace their baldness and go completely bald. Some women, especially if they opt for a shorter haircut, will switch to wearing wigs exclusively.

People who have trichotillomania naturally benefit from using hair replacement therapy in a way that best suits their situation. It especially benefits people who have severe forms of trichotillomania, in cases where they may have created several balding or thinning patches of hair on their scalp.

Some people may be given medications to induce hair growth if they have severe trichotillomania and are attempting to successfully regulate their hair tearing or yanking. Since it's non-surgical, it's a safer and simpler way for people to get started rehabilitating their scalp.

Others with trichotillomania do get surgery as a form of hair replacement therapy, though it's a little riskier, especially if they're still recovering from behaviors, such as tearing out their hair. While some people do stop tearing out their hair after getting surgery, others might not. That's why it's important to talk to your doctor and/or therapist about the best course of action to take regarding surgical hair replacement therapy.

Trichotillomania And Alternative Treatment

People who have trichotillomania don't always have to rely on conventional treatment options. In fact, there are a number of alternative treatment options they can use instead. Hypnosis, as an example, is probably one of the more prevalent forms of treatment for various psychological disorders.

The Case With Hypnosis

Hypnosis, also known as hypnotic suggestion or hypnotherapy, is a practice where a patient is induced into a trance-like state that causes them to gain heightened concentration and focus. A hypnotherapist is the practitioner that induces or lulls the patient in a trance-like state; once the patient enters this trance-like state, they become much more calm, relaxed and open to the hypnotherapist's suggestions.

Hypnosis is used to treat various psychological conditions. It's mainly used as a way for people to gain control over any of their undesirable behaviors, especially if those behaviors dominate various aspects of their live. It's also an effective way to cope with both anxiety and stress before medical procedures and throughout one's daily life, particularly if one or the other are severe.

The use of hypnosis as a treatment has been researched for years. Thanks to that research, we now know that hypnosis may play a role in helping:

- **Behavior changes** – Hypnosis has been successfully utilized for the treatment of problematic behaviors like insomnia, smoking, phobias and overeating (obesity).
- **Hot flashes** – Some women may benefit from using hypnosis to curb pre-menopausal and post-menopausal symptoms like hot flashes.
- **Pain control** – The use of hypnosis is known to provide some benefits for curbing pain associated

with conditions like cancer, headaches and medical procedures.

When used to treat trichotillomania, hypnosis may be effective in helping people identify and eliminate their negative thoughts. It also helps people who have trichotillomania eventually replace their repetitious hair tearing or yanking behaviors with other positive behaviors that may break their cycle of negative behaviors.

Other Alternative Treatments

People who have trichotillomania also use other alternative treatments to effectively manage the disorder. Relaxation techniques, such as massages, meditation and progressive muscle relaxation help people who have trichotillomania curb their desire to tug or pluck out hairs on their scalp and body.

These techniques revolve around relaxing the body as much as possible, which allows people to eliminate the stress, anxiety and negativity that may cause them to start tearing or yanking out their hair.

Other alternative treatments like acupuncture and herbal supplementation have been used for treating trichotillomania, but they don't yet have substantial evidence supporting them as effective treatments. Despite that, it doesn't hurt to safely experiment with alternative trichotillomania treatments to see if they work well in treating the condition.

Choosing The Right Treatment

No two people who have trichotillomania will ever get the same treatment. If they do happen to get the same treatment, they'll ultimately react to it in very different ways.

What's the best trichotillomania treatment for you? Ultimately, the best treatment for you will be the one that matches your specific needs. Just think about how many people experiment with behavioral therapy, medication therapy, hair replacement therapy and other forms of therapy to find one treatment that works for their trichotillomania.

Some people don't find a solution until they combine several treatments into an entire treatment plan. Of course, many people also rely on the assistance of their doctor and/or psychiatrist for additional help.

Some treatments benefit other people better — that especially applies to people of different ages. Children, as an example, are known to benefit more from undergoing therapy for trichotillomania, since it's considered safer than merely using medications. Adults, on the other hand, can benefit from using a combination of therapies and medication to get the best possible results out of their treatment plan.

People who have other underlying physical or mental conditions should also consider treatments that won't negatively impact these conditions. This is important because some treatments and therapies might harm one's mental or physical state more than actually help it.

Treating trichotillomania is considered a hassle, but it doesn't have to be. That's something important to keep in mind whether you're treating trichotillomania exclusively or as a symptom of another underlying condition.

Chapter 4: Managing And Coping With Trichotillomania

It's completely possible to cope with trichotillomania. In most cases, it's just as easy to manage trichotillomania and live with the condition. That's pretty much the goal of any trichotillomania treatment—and it should be your goal if you're struggling with the condition.

In this section of our book, we're going to take a closer look at how people actually manage trichotillomania and cope with some of the symptoms that make the condition seem entirely hopeless. But, managing trichotillomania isn't hopeless, as long as you understand how to cope with the condition.

Dealing With Trichotillomania

One of the most important aspects of dealing with trichotillomania is learning how to understand yourself. Although it sounds a little too generalized, it's probably one of the biggest themes of trichotillomania treatment, especially psychotherapy treatments used for managing and relieving symptoms from trichotillomania.

Understanding yourself, in the context of trichotillomania, mainly involves learning why you yank out your hair in the first place. You might want to ask yourself:

- What do I feel when I pull out my hair?
- What sensory needs do I fulfill when I pull out my hair?

- What actions or feelings fuel my hair pulling urges?
- What triggers my hair pulling urges?

If you can answer one or several of those questions, you'll likely get closer to understanding more about why you might feel compelled to compulsively pull out your hair. Reaching that step is perhaps the first step in making a successful start in any trichotillomania treatment plan.

You might learn that you pluck your hair for cosmetic reasons. This especially applies to people who tend to pluck hair on other parts of their body, including their face. Some people pluck their hair because they desire some form of perfection—a form of perfection that's unattainable because it's *unhealthy*.

The aforementioned reasons make people develop the hair yanking habits defining trichotillomania. Though, many of those reasons also define the triggers that make people act out, too.

Triggers are certain words, phrases or topics that immediately cause people emotional distress. They typically make people recount traumatic experiences, but they also invoke certain emotions in people, such as anger or distress.

When it comes to psychological disorders, triggers define the 'little things' that make people behave in a certain way, whether they're reacting physically or emotionally. Something as innocuous as a book passage could make a person feel distressed or compelled to start partaking in a destructive behavior. It also applies to the things that people may say or do around the person whose emotions may become triggered.

People who have trichotillomania also have triggers that may make them immediately start pulling their hair. Triggers for trichotillomania are either physical or emotional.

Sometimes, a person with trichotillomania may start tugging out their hair when they're sitting still or doing something. The physical trigger, in this case, would be their need to do something with their hands while occupied with another activity.

People who have trichotillomania may feel compelled to tear out their hair when they're under incredible stress or anxiety. That's one of the most prevalent emotional triggers for people who have the disorder. When they feel compelled to tear their hair, they have to do it immediately, so they can relieve the negative emotions plaguing them.

Writing each time you feel like tugging out your hair works, too. Not only can you record each instance where you feel like tugging out your hair, but you can also include the thoughts and/or feelings accompanying your urges to tug out your hair. In addition, write down what's happening at that exact moment when you feel the need to forcibly tug your hair and note how severe the urge is.

You can even show your health care provider to give them some insight into how your issues with trichotillomania work 'behind the scenes.'

Keeping a diary about your trichotillomania urges does help health providers find better treatment options specifically tailored to treating your instance of trichotillomania. Of course, it takes time to find a health care provider with experience treating people who compulsively tug out their hair. It's best to stick with a health care provider (like a therapist) who knows how to effectively treat people who have trichotillomania.

Dealing With Recovery

Recovering from any condition is hard. For some people, it can get tricky. However, as long as we keep our priorities in order, we'll be able to make a full recovery from any condition, including trichotillomania.

Some people assume that trichotillomania is hard to treat, mainly due to the repetitive nature of the disorder. The repetitive nature of hair tearing or yanking, as mentioned throughout this book, often gets to a point where it's an unbreakable cycle. Many people feel trapped by trichotillomania, as a result of that cycle.

Though, there's a way to get through recovery. If you believe you can get through recovery, you'll be able to make great progress throughout the entire process.

Don't believe it? You really can't accomplish much if you don't believe you can accomplish anything. That same idea applies to recovering from various disorders like trichotillomania.

Without having some belief in overcoming those harmful and addictive behaviors, it's difficult to learn new behaviors to replace them. In other words, it's possible to lose confidence in yourself, when recovering from a condition like trichotillomania. You'll lose your priorities and instead focus on negative things that ultimately stunt your recovery.

Of course, you'll feel upset and frustrated with the recovery process. But, hear us out. It takes time to recover from any disorder. You're not going to 'get better' overnight. Focusing on your trichotillomania treatment plan should be your main priority, so you can eventually get on a clear road to recovery. If you don't believe in yourself, it gets pretty hard to stay on track.

A Good Support System

Having a good support system is one of the most important parts of the recovery process. Many people, in fact, thrive on having a good support system to make them feel better about making their journey to recovery. People just don't feel motivated enough to make any changes... if they don't have someone cheering for them along the way.

Family and friends make good support systems. They're especially important for children and teenagers who have trichotillomania. Having people close to them encouraging them throughout treatment does wonders for the state of their self-esteem, arguably boosting their inclination to make a full recovery from their harmful behaviors.

Health care providers also make another worthy part of a good support system. Your mental and physical health care providers should communicate with each other about your recovery process, particularly if your treatment options intersect with one another.

If you don't happen to have a strong network of family or friends, support groups for trichotillomania exist. You can search online for various online forums and social media hangouts for people who have or have recovered from trichotillomania. We'll even list the most popular trichotillomania resources at the end of this book.

You can look locally for trichotillomania support groups. Sometimes, you can even check in with habit disorder support groups, as many people who have trichotillomania exhibit many of the same symptoms as people who have other habit disorders. Of course, you can look for local trichotillomania support groups online, but it doesn't hurt to browse classified advertisements in a newspaper, either.

Having someone to talk to makes the recovery process much easier — and a lot less lonely. The key to making a full recovery is all about receiving enough encouragement to feel confident in getting better. That alone is the key to effectively utilizing trichotillomania treatment.

Getting Started With Managing Trichotillomania

We've talked about learning how to cope with trichotillomania in the last two sections. Though, we haven't yet looked at trichotillomania management from the perspective of different age groups. As we've mentioned throughout this book, people of all ages develop trichotillomania. It typically starts from a young age, but only really 'sticks around' as a disordered habit the older you are.

There are several specified treatment plans for people of different ages: children, teenagers and adults. In this section, we're going to take a look at three specific treatment 'regimes' that apply to children, teens and adults — in that order.

Managing Trichotillomania In Children

One of the most important things for parents to understand is that it's not their fault that their child has trichotillomania. Instead of shifting blame on yourself about your child's disorder, it's more important to find ways to effectively help your child overcome the disorder. Accept that your child has trichotillomania (in some form) and help them overcome it by accepting it by giving them unconditional acceptance.

How trichotillomania affects children depends on their age. A child's age even determines whether their trichotillomania is temporary or a milder form of the disorder. Let's look at how trichotillomania affects children of different age groups:

- **Babies** (1 month to 2 years old) – At this age, babies typically tug out their hair as a self-comforting habit.

It's usually paired with thumb-sucking as a repetitive behavior. When they recline or lie down, they typically sit with their thumb or fingers in the mouth; with their other hand, they twist and/or tug their hair or even their mother's hair. Babies usually find this behavior relaxing, and often engage themselves in this behavior when they feel distressed or sleepy.

- **Toddlers** (2 to 5 years old) – Children who tugged their (or their mother's) hair as babies will continue doing it as toddlers. They even start doing the action automatically, and without thinking about it. By the time they're age 3, they'll start understanding how their parents react to their hair tugging behaviors. If they see that their parents react to their hair tugging, they'll start hair tugging as additional 'leverage' for getting parental attention. Younger toddlers typically twist their hair, while younger ones pluck.

- **School Age** (5 to 12 years) – During this stage of their lives, children will start developing trichotillomania in different ways. Some children yank their hair as a habit or in response to anger. Other children, however, start pulling their hair out of anxiety or stress. When that happens, the child may be developing some form of trichotillomania due to that source of stress. Many children in this age group also have trouble expressing how they feel, so they might even hide the fact that they're tearing out their hair. Parents need to talk to their school-age children to ensure they understand and support them if they need help coping with and managing their trichotillomania.

- **Adolescent** (12 to 18 years) – This age group is more

likely to outright develop trichotillomania in some form. In fact, many adolescents in this age group are more prone to developing habit disorders like obsessive-compulsive disorder. Teens who already tug their hair will continue to tug their hair, usually out of a response to stress, if they don't get treatment. Due to this, it's important for parents to talk to their child and provide them support throughout the recovery process.

Some children end up tearing or plucking out their hair due to anger or frustration, otherwise known as acting out for parental attention. Others, however, start tearing their hair out of a need for relief from stress or anxiety that they don't quite understand. Many of those children later go on to keep tearing or plucking out their hair well into their teens and even adulthood.

When it comes to helping children manage trichotillomania in some form, it's important to identify where their sources of stress may originate.

If you have a child struggling with trichotillomania, it's important to stay completely communicative with them about their disorder. Children always need support, especially when dealing with a disorder as serious as trichotillomania. If you're there for them, they'll feel more confident about undergoing treatment and making a full recovery.

A trichotillomania management plan for children generally involves steps that help curb problematic behaviors that may lead to hair yanking. Targeting high risk 'hair yanking times' is one example of utilizing a trichotillomania management plan for a child. When you pinpoint what time your child engages in that behavior, you can take immediate action to help them learn positive and healthier behaviors.

Other ideas for managing trichotillomania in children include giving them a shorter haircut or a hair cap to sleep in. Some parents cover their little ones' hands in gloves or mittens before they touch their hair during 'high risk' hair yanking times. Others give their children objects, like feathers or ribbons, to keep their mind occupied before they start pulling their hair.

Managing Trichotillomania In Teens And Adults

Both teens and adults share similar issues with managing their trichotillomania, so we've kept both treatment plans in the same section to highlight their similarities.

Many teens with trichotillomania end up 'keeping' the disorder well into adulthood, usually because they don't seek any kind of treatment that would help them curb the symptoms of the disorder.

That continues into adulthood, too, especially if they think trichotillomania isn't worth treating. When trichotillomania gets so invasive that it affects your life, that's when you need to do something to curb the persistent symptoms of the disorder.

Teens And Trichotillomania

Most teens develop habit disorders out of a need to curb both stress and anxiety. Teens are likely to develop habit disorders or impulse control disorders, due to the fact that they're exposed to more sources of stress and anxiety, namely from school settings. Teens with trichotillomania start tearing or yanking their hair due to that reason, and the behaviors eventually get to a point where they're nearly uncontrollable.

Teens with trichotillomania are also likely to have an underlying disorder, such as anxiety, depression or problems with their self image. Those reasons, coupled with the fact that teens tend to be a lot more secretive than children, define why treating trichotillomania in teens can be rather tricky.

Teens need focused attention, especially when it comes to treating psychological disorders. Teenagers tend to have a difficult time breaking bad habits if they don't have guidance in helping them develop newer, more positive habits.

That reason is one reason why therapy tends to be a common form of treatment for teens with trichotillomania. Therapists help teenagers evaluate and learn more information about how their hair tugging habit formed, in addition to learning how to break those bad habits. Some teens are even prescribed medications for treating the disorder (in addition to any other underlying disorders).

Trichotillomania In Adults ~ Coping With Trichotillomania

We know that adults more or less inherit trichotillomania from childhood and adolescence. Now, it's time to see how adults (and teens) can cope with managing their disorder.

As mentioned, the most essential part of recognizing trichotillomania as a disorder is identifying its physical signs and behavioral signs. After that, it's best to learn more about the disorder and what makes it tick. But, after you learn all you can about the disorder, how can you apply what you learned to actually finding a way to treat your trichotillomania?

As an adult or teenager, there are several things you can do:

Keep a journal or chart recording your episodes. As mentioned in the last section, writing down details about your hair pulling episodes will let you actually 'see' how often your episodes occur. It's best to write down the time, date, location and number of hairs. Don't forget to include what you used to yank out those hairs.

Writing down your thoughts and feelings also helps put your hair pulling episodes into perspective—not to mention, it helps get rid of any lingering negative feelings you might have about having trichotillomania. Besides writing about your episodes, write out a list of immediate and long-term consequences of hair tearing or yanking. In fact, write down a list of the consequences that directly affect you due to your episodes. You can make a list for work, home, social events and even school, if you still attend.

Develop a plan to start controlling your episodes. In this book, we've talked about various solutions to help people who have trichotillomania stop tearing or yanking out their hair. That doesn't mean you can't develop a plan on your own.

There's a popular behavioral plan that teaches people how to notice, stop and choose a plan for regulating problematic repetitive behaviors. This plan consists of noticing when you develop an uncontrollable desire to rip out your hair, stopping the urge from happening and then choosing a plan for suppressing those urges, such as listening to positive reminders in your head as the urge bothers you.

Try keeping little notes around your home or workplace with reminders to stop pulling your hair. This is especially helpful for people who have specific places where they tend to experience hair tearing or yanking episodes. Another way you can stifle your desire to tear your hair out is delegating your attention to something else:

- Taking a few moments to clear your mind of any thoughts.
- Drawing, painting, writing and/or scribbling on a blank piece of paper
- Listening to music, especially music appealing to your emotions
- Playing video games or watching television
- Calling or talking to a friend online
- Volunteering or socializing with community groups,

such as a trichotillomania support group.

Sometimes, wearing a physical barrier can help 'train' you to stop yanking out your hair. That usually involves wearing ankle weights on your arm or a rubber glove. The weights weigh down on your arm whenever you attempt to lift your arm toward your head, making it difficult to reach your hair.

Of course, it's even more important to reduce any source of stress around you. Many people, including teenagers, tear out their hair because they're stressed, tired or anxious about various aspects of their lives. Eliminating those sources of stress make managing your trichotillomania symptoms much easier.

Relaxation exercises, as we've mentioned in a previous section, are a popular stress reducing activity. Progressive body relaxation exercises, such as progressive muscle relaxation, help relax the muscles and the rest of the body. That helps release a lot of stress and tension welled up within the body.

→ Progressive muscle relaxation

Progressive muscle relaxation may help people who have trichotillomania cope with relieving sources of stress that can provoke their behaviors.

Many progressive muscle relaxation exercises involve tensing one of the body's muscle groups as you inhale and then relaxing them as you breathe out. Due to the nature of these exercises, each muscle group can be worked in any order.

It takes weeks to completely adjust to a progressive muscle relaxation routine. The more you do the exercise, the easier it becomes to make your body slip into a state of near complete relaxation. By then, it becomes a pretty effective stress reliever.

Some people use calming, meditative or relaxing music to put themselves into the mood before and during their exercises. You can find many relaxing or meditative music mixes online and in music stores.

Of course, progressive muscle relaxation exercises aren't an immediate 'cure' for trichotillomania symptoms, but it helps alleviate stress that may provoke hair tearing.

Activities like yoga, martial arts and other forms of aerobic exercise help a lot, and let's not forget about meditation, too.

→ Trichotillomania and mediation

Meditation is a tried and true stress reliever—after all, it's been practiced for thousands of years. The practice is considered a type of mind-body medicine, one that complements the well being of both mind and body. As a result, many meditation techniques make people enter a deep state of relaxation and maintain a peaceful mind.

Meditation makes people focus their attention and eliminate the thoughts clouding their mind — thoughts that often cause stress and anxiety. Ultimately, meditation helps people maintain a sense of peace and calm that benefits their health.

When used as a form of treatment for trichotillomania, it helps eliminate the stress and anxiety that might provoke hair plucking sessions. Focusing your attention and breathing deeply (in a relaxed setting) is the simplest way to meditate if you need to 'cool off' from negative thoughts and emotions.

Although it takes time to get used to meditation as a stress reliever, it's incredibly helpful in times of need. There are many meditation resources on the web and in libraries that can help you get started.

Of course, your self-esteem influences the effectiveness of any trichotillomania treatment you try. In a previous section, we stressed the importance of believing in yourself in order to overcome your hair tearing habits. That applies here, too.

If you don't believe in yourself, it's difficult to stay motivated. That's pretty much the truth. If your morale, confidence and self-esteem have taken a hit, it's time to build them back up again, so you can get back on the track to recovery.

Sometimes, writing down a list of your accomplishments, strengths and favorite things can help boost your morale. It doesn't hurt to look at things that you legitimately love watching, reading and listening to, as well.

Remember this: **only you can make your recovery happen**. It's pretty easy to read about eliminating your trichotillomania symptoms and habits, but it's even harder to implement those suggestions in your daily life. In order to successfully incorporate those suggestions into your daily life, **believe you can do it**. It's the only way.

Trichotillomania might be an uncommon impulse control disorder, but it affects millions across the country – and the rest of the world – every day. We hope our book did some good in helping you make a change to fight, and eventually overcome, your life with trichotillomania.

Resources

If you would like some worksheets rather than take up space in this book you can print them off directly from

http://global.oup.com/us/companion.websites/umbrella/treatments/hidden/pdf/Worksheets_forms.pdf
http://goo.gl/ytshg5

Welcome to the Trichotillomania Learning Center
http://www.trich.org/

Find a Support Group – the Trichotillomania Learning Center
http://www.trich.org/treatment/support-groups.html

Online Resources – the Trichotillomania Learning Center
http://www.trich.org/treatment/resources-online.html

For Kids & Teens – the Trichotillomania Learning Center
http://www.trich.org/about/for-kids-teens.html

Trichotillomania – Medscape Reference
http://emedicine.medscape.com/article/1071854-overview

Trichotillomania Support
http://www.trichotillomania.co.uk/

Trich in Schools – Trichotillomania Support
http://www.trichotillomania.co.uk/Parents/school.htm

StopPulling.com, *the only interactive program for trichotillomania available*
http://stoppulling.com

Pinterest.com
http://www.pinterest.com/madiibeekirby/trichotillomania-stuff/

Worksheets

The best resource I have found for worksheets that you can use straight away (and print out for free) is from

http://global.oup.com/us/companion.websites/umbrella/treatments/hidden/pdf/Worksheets_forms.pdf

Or simply type in - **bit.ly/1pbz9uM** and it will take you to the same page.

Conclusion

Thank you again for downloading this book!

Trichotillomania may be uncommon and considered 'difficult to treat,' but the strategies and advice provided in this book can help you overcome the disorder, one step at a time.

Overcoming a disorder like trichotillomania takes hard work, but if you believe you can accomplish it, it won't be as hard as you think. Take some time to remember the information we've provided in this book before you take the next step in your recovery.

The next step is to look up more information about trichotillomania and get started changing your life!

Finally, if you enjoyed this book, please take the time to share your thoughts and post a review on Amazon. It would be greatly appreciated!

onychophagia, 10